THE PATTERN OF THIS WORLD

SIX STUDIES ON THE CHRISTIAN AND THE MEDIA

ROGER FAWCETT

CF4·K

10 9 8 7 6 5 4 3 2 1

ISBN: 978-1-84550-644-5

Edited by David Jackman and Thalia Blundell

Published in 2011 by
Christian Focus Publications, Geanies House, Fearn,
Tain, Ross-shire, IV20 1TW, Great Britain.
www.christianfocus.com
Cover design by Paul Lewis
Printed by Bell and Bain, Glasgow

CONTENTS

INTRODUCTION 4

SERIES OVERVIEW 16

LESSON 1 – GOD AND YOUR HEART
(1 JOHN 1:8 – 2:2; 2:15-17) 19

LESSON 2 – GOD AND YOUR MIND
(ROMANS 11:32 – 12:2) 26

LESSON 3 – GOD AND YOUR EYES
(LUKE 11:29-36) 34

LESSON 4 – GOD AND YOUR WORDS
(COLOSSIANS 4:2-6, EPHESIANS 4:25-29, 5:4) ... 43

LESSON 5 – GOD AND YOUR HANDS
(PROVERBS 6:6-11) 51

LESSON 6 – GOD AND YOUR LIFE
(EPHESIANS 5:1-16) 59

WORKSHEETS 68

INTRODUCTION

BY NICK MARGESSON

As a youth leader you have the great privilege of introducing young people to the Lord Jesus Christ and helping them to grow in the Christian faith. The 14-18s age group are at the junction between the younger teens and the adult church and this is often where we lose them. *The Junction* is a series of books designed to help you teach older teens to study the Bible in a way which is challenging and intellectually stretching. Because they are often unprepared to take things at face value and are encouraged to question everything, it is important to satisfy the mind while touching the heart. The ready-to-use sessions contained in the books are for youth groups of varying sizes, with normal leaders and normal teenagers who want to serve an awesome God.

Each book in the series contains one teaching module, which will normally last from 4-7 weeks. At the front of the book is an overview of the Bible teaching, which can be photocopied for your church leader so that he/she is aware of what is being taught. Each lesson plan, in addition to a lesson aim, contains study notes to enable the leader to understand the Bible passage, a slot to encourage the young people to share experiences and learn from each other, a suggestion to focus attention on the study to follow, suggestions for a prayer and praise time and an optional worksheet to help the young people engage with the passage. Recognising that youth groups vary in size and available space, every effort has been made to include activities that are easily adaptable.

Putting Together a Youth Group Session

What should we include in our youth group sessions?

If you wander into any Christian bookshop and ask the question, 'What should we include in our youth group sessions?' you had better be prepared for a very long stay in the bookshop! Just about every book on youth ministry that you pick up off the shelf will give you a different answer to that question – generally based on the author's preference, upbringing, experiences, etc. Interestingly, if you pick up your Bible and ask the same question you will also be in for a long wait, because, as far as I can see, the Bible never mentions youth groups, let alone what might be involved in a youth group session. In fact, the Bible very rarely makes any distinction between particular groupings of Christians – it talks about all Christians and makes no particular distinction about age or nationality or background, etc.

So, if our youth group is a Christian youth group, then the question we really need to ask is, 'What does it look like when Christians (of any age) get together?' And, on this subject, the Bible has plenty to say! One of the most complete descriptions of what this looks like in practice comes in Acts 2:42-47, where we are given a fairly detailed description of what the earliest group of believers was like. Whenever God's people got together, they engaged in a whole variety of activities – they prayed together, they praised God together, they learned from God's word together, they reminded each other of what God had done for them, they cared practically for each other, they spent plenty of time together, they cared for the world around them, they proclaimed the good news of Jesus, and so on. You could sum it up by saying that they were devoted to God and devoted to each other. And, interestingly, this type of devotion was clearly very attractive to the world around them – 'the Lord added to their number daily those who were being saved' (Acts 2:47).

If our youth group is a Christian youth group then, in a youth appropriate way, we need to be displaying that same devotion to God and to each other whenever we meet together. What elements in our youth group sessions will help our groups to do this?

- **Time** – it is noticeable in Acts 2 how much time the early believers spent together. They met together daily in the temple courts, they ate together, they hung out at each others' homes.

  With busy teenagers and busy leaders, spending this much time together would be impossible for just about every youth group, but relationships are a key element of being devoted to one another, and relationships need time and space to develop. In our programming we need to allow time and space for young people and leaders to hang out together.

  Food is a great way to get people to spend time together and, again, it does not have to be complicated or fancy – a bag of doughnuts or some cheese toasties or a pizza are not difficult to arrange.

  In the session outlines in this material, we have not included hang-out time because the way it works best will be different for each group. The hang-out time does not have to be particularly structured but it does need to happen.

- **Teaching** – in Acts 2 we are told that the believers devoted themselves to the Apostles' teaching (verse 42). The Apostles were commissioned by Jesus to be the authoritative teachers of the early church (John 15:26-27). In the New Testament, the Apostles' teaching is authenticated as God's word through signs and wonders (Acts 2:43).

  Of course, today, we have the amazing privilege of being able to listen to the Apostles' teaching and so listen to God's word whenever the Bible is opened and read and studied. Being devoted to God must, at least, mean listening to his word and trying to put it into practice in our lives. This is why really good Bible teaching needs to be at the centre of our youth group sessions.

  In the session outlines in this material, the 'Bible Time' is one of the key elements to the session. There will usually be a couple of components to the 'Bible Time' – an introductory Bible activity (Focus) followed by a short Bible study.

  For more help on teaching the Bible to young people, please see 'Seven top tips for teaching the Bible to young people' on page 10.

- **Sharing and Testimony** – one of the ways that Christians show that they are devoted to one another is by getting to know one another and by listening and learning from each other. In our youth group sessions it is great to be able to programme in times where people can get to know each other a bit better. That might be by running a simple mixer activity or by interviewing somebody or by asking people to share their experiences or thoughts on a particular topic or issue.

  In the session outlines in this material we have included a 'Talk Time' in each session. Sometimes these 'Talk Times' are specifically linked to the teaching topic for that session and sometimes they just refer to general issues facing Christians.

We have also included an optional 'Getting to Know You' slot in each session. If your group members already know each other really well then you may decide that this activity is unnecessary.

- **Prayer** – One of the most foundational activities that Christians engage in when they meet together is prayer. Prayer reflects our common status as forgiven sinners who are dependent on God. Prayer demonstrates our concern for and commitment to one another. And yet prayer is often one of the first things that gets dropped from a youth group session or from the programme generally – usually because praying together is embarrassing or hard work. If our groups are Christian groups then we need to pray together and for one another. In fact, although it can be hard work getting a group praying, one of the best ways to grow in devotion to one another is by praying together.

  In the session outlines in this material we have included a 'Prayer Time' in each session. Sometimes this prayer time is directed and flows out of the Bible teaching; sometimes the prayer time is more general.

- **Praising God** – right at the heart of what it means to be Christian, both individually and corporately, is praising God. The psalmist overflows with praise to God, so do the early Christians in Acts 2, and so should the young people in our youth groups.

  Whenever young people meet together as Christians, they ought to be reminded of what God has done and encouraged to praise him. This may mean singing together, but for groups that would prefer not to sing, it will mean exploring other ways to express praise to God – perhaps in reading a Psalm together.

In the session outlines in this material we have included a 'Praise Time' in every session, and have made suggestions for both musical and non-musical youth groups.

- **Practical Care** – probably the most striking and challenging aspect of the early believers' life together, as described in Acts 2, is the practical care that they show for one another: 'All the believers were together and had everything in common. Selling their possessions and goods, they gave to anyone as he had need.'

  This practical and material care for each other ought to be reflected in all Christian youth groups, but rarely seems to be (in the western world at least). We need to give serious thought to how we care for one another practically and how that expresses itself in a youth group environment.

  In the session outlines in this material, we have not included suggestions for practical care because the way it works best will be different for each group, but practical care is an important part of what it means to be Christians together and we need to make sure that it is happening in our groups.

Seven Top Tips for Teaching the Bible to Young People

Tip 1 – Pray

It is God's word that we are teaching so we need his help to teach it. Ultimately he is the only one who can open our eyes to understand the Bible and open the eyes of the young people in our youth groups. So we need to pray when we are preparing, and while we are teaching and afterwards, that God would be at work through the Holy Spirit, helping people to listen, understand and put into practice what we are hearing from God's word.

Tip 2 – The Bible must set the agenda

If we are going to teach the Bible properly to young people we need to let the Bible do the teaching. We need to make sure that what we are teaching in a youth group session is what the passage teaches, and not what we, as the leaders, want to teach or what we think the young people need to hear.

Obviously, as we have planned the programme or picked the topics, we will have had some ideas about why we are teaching that particular topic, but when it actually comes down to dealing with the passage, we need to teach what it says and not what we want it to say. And we need to make sure that all of the elements that go to make up a youth group session work together in teaching the passage.

Tip 3 – Be clear without compromising

The key to good communication is clarity – see Nehemiah 8:8. And the key to clarity is knowing what you want to teach and working out how to teach it in a way that is appropriate, understandable and memorable.

Please note: teaching clearly is not the same as being simplistic or dumbing-down; even the most difficult or complicated truths can be taught to young people if they are taught clearly. Inevitably this means that a good amount of work needs to be done in preparation to make sure that you, as the teacher, understand a passage or a topic. After all, if we do not understand a passage or a topic clearly, then what hope do we have of teaching it clearly to others?

Having done the hard work of understanding a passage or topic, we need then to think carefully about how we communicate that to our target audience. It is a useful exercise to ask whether we are teaching in a way that is appropriate, understandable and memorable.

Tip 4 – Good relationships help good teaching

It is generally true to say that good relationships facilitate good communication – see 1 Thessalonians 2:8. Of course, it is possible to communicate perfectly effectively with a complete stranger, but it is fair to say that, in normal circumstances, communication is easier where there is a good relationship in place. For instance, in trying to work out what level of communication is appropriate (see above) it helps to know the young people with whom we are trying to communicate, particularly in terms of language, illustration and application.

Some things to remember about developing relationships with young people:

- **Make the Effort**

Building relationships with young people takes time and effort, so we need to make sure that there is enough space in our programme for relationships to develop.

- **Make Boundaries**

Relationships flourish where there are clear and consistently enforced boundaries. It is possible to fall into the trap of thinking that being friends with a young person means allowing them to do what they like or never telling them off. Adult friendships do not work like that and neither do relationships between adults and young people. Young people need to know 'where they stand'; they need to feel secure in relationships and sometimes that means being firm in terms of discipline, boundaries, etc.

- **Be Yourself**

Young people want to relate to adults, so be yourself and do not try to be a teenager. Young people have plenty of friends of their own age, but what many are looking for, particularly in the transition between child and adult, is adults who will value and take an interest in them. Many teenagers, particularly if they are going through a period of conflict or non-communication with their parents, will look for supportive relationships with other adults. Interestingly, this relationship is often developed with a grandparent.

This means that youth and children's leaders do not have to pretend to be younger than they are. It also means that when we are putting together teams to work with children and young people, we do not have to limit ourselves to young leaders.

- **Listen**

Genuine relationships are two-way. So, in building relationships with young people, we need to listen and be appropriately honest and open. Paul talks about sharing his life with the Thessalonians (1 Thessalonians 2:8).

- **Do not take yourself too seriously!**

Because relationships are two-way, there is a possibility that we, as leaders, will be let down in a relationship. This is often the case with teenagers, who may not attach the same importance and significance to a relationship, so it is important that adult leaders do not take themselves too seriously.

Tip 5 – Be aware of the culture but not a slave to it

There is a school of thought that says that those who are involved in youth and children's work have to immerse themselves in the culture of young people – live how they live, dress how they dress, do what they do, etc. That is NOT what is being suggested here. Quite apart from anything else, youth culture is extremely difficult to define, partly because it is a mixture of all sorts of cultures and partly because no young person willingly fits into the 'typical' category.

There are, however, clearly differences between the world of young people and the world of adults. But, as we have seen already, young people want to relate to adults, and are therefore expecting that there will be a degree of cultural diversity. In fact, it is often this cultural diversity which adds value to the relationship – the fact that someone from a different world, culturally, is taking an interest in me and my world.

Having said all that, taking an interest in their lives and the world in which they live is an indication that we care for people, so it is worth being aware of the culture of the young people with whom we are working. So we might not like the music that they are into, but we can still ask about it. We may not watch the same programmes that they like, but we can still be aware of them.

In particular, if we are trying to communicate to teenagers, then it is worth learning about communication in the world of young people. Obviously, as we spend time with young people, we will begin to learn how they communicate.

However, there are a couple of ways that you can short-cut the process:

- Talk to school teachers. They are the ones who are specifically trained to communicate to young people. Good school teachers will have a wealth of knowledge and experience in communicating to teenagers.
- Watch television – particularly early in the evening, when programming and advertising is aimed specifically at young people. It is worth watching the advertisements every now and again, because advertisers know how to communicate to teenagers.

Tip 6 – Be varied in communication

One of the lessons from the culture of young people is the need to use variety in our communication. A very quick look at the advertisements or morning television shows us that young people are used to receiving a great deal of information, very quickly. And that information comes in a variety of forms – images, noises, words, instructions, actions, etc. Being varied in communication recognises, as we have seen already, that people learn or take in information differently.

Of course the Bible itself is full of variety in communication. Sometimes the communication is very visual – dreams, visions, parables or exciting narrative. Even as we read the passages, we are encouraged to visualise what is happening. Sometimes the communication is audible – the prophet speaks, the letter is read out, Jesus talks to somebody – and, again, even as we read these passages, it is as though we are listening in to what is being said. Sometimes the communication in the Bible is more physical – animal sacrifice, Jesus touching the leper, Thomas touching Jesus' hands and side, all communicating theological truth physically.

When teaching the Bible to young people it is important that we allow the richness and diversity of the Bible to be reflected in our teaching.

Tip 7 – Preparation is everything

Preparing a youth group session can be harder than preparing a talk or a study for adults. As well as doing all of the same preparation in terms of understanding the passage, you then have to work out how on earth you are going to communicate it to 14, 16, or 18 year olds.

The more time that leaders are able to take in preparing sessions, the better able they will be to teach young people effectively.

SERIES OVERVIEW

THE PATTERN OF THIS WORLD

Lesson 1 **God and Your Heart** .... I John 1:8 – 2:2; 2:15-17
Love for God conflicts with love for the world. There is only one number one in your life.

Lesson 2 **God and Your Mind** .... Romans 11:32 – 12:2
A transformed heart leads to a transformed mind. Don't be squeezed by the world any longer.

Lesson 3 **God and Your Eyes** .... Luke 11:29-36
A transformed heart leads to healthy eyes. Fix your eyes on Jesus and his teaching to counteract the darkness of the world.

Lesson 4 **God and Your Words** .... Colossians 4:2-6, Ephesians 4:25-29; 5:4
A transformed heart leads to speech full of grace. Spice your conversation with the salt of the gospel.

Lesson 5 **God and Your Hands** .... Proverbs 6:6-11
A transformed heart leads to working hands. Don't be a screen junkie.

Lesson 6 **God and Your Life** .... Ephesians 5:1-16
A transformed heart leads to a changed life. Don't compartmentalise your life.

This course was written in response to requests from leaders and young people for something on social media and the internet – which is a pretty big topic and therefore quite a tall order to cover in six sessions. It is, of course, impossible to write something that will cover every aspect that every group wants to talk about, so in these studies much of the emphasis for the leaders will be on letting the discussion go in the direction that the young people want/need it to.

Another problem with starting to write a Bible Study series about the media and trying to crowbar everything in is that our agenda is set the wrong way round. An issue arises amongst the group, e.g. someone has pressed 'send' on an MSN message that they really shouldn't have sent, the topic is chosen ('Next week the study will be "What the Bible says about MSN"') and the leader spends the intervening week scouring the internet (ironically!) for anything anybody has written about social networking and the Bible. Problem: our agenda is set by the world and we are reactive.

The solution is to let the Bible set the agenda and to be proactive in meeting the different issues head on. Whilst the Bible doesn't mention our modern technologies and challenges, it still has much to say that can be applied to those situations. These studies focus on six Bible passages that challenge us to live for Jesus in different areas of our lives. As the Bible sets the agenda for our obedience to Christ, in response to his saving grace for us, we will begin to realise the importance of thinking through every aspect of our lives, especially where we encounter the media.

Another problem with a study such as this is application. It will be very difficult to give hard and fast guidelines and there will be many different attitudes and levels of experience within the group. Romans 14 begins:

> 1 Accept him whose faith is weak, without passing judgment on disputable
> matters. 2 One man's faith allows him to eat everything, but another man,
> whose faith is weak, eats only vegetables. 3 The man who eats everything
> must not look down on him who does not, and the man who does not eat
> everything must not condemn the man who does, for God has accepted him.

Here is the challenge for the older and more mature members of the group, to be humble and perhaps work with younger members in helping them with their different struggles. These studies are not the time to blandly state, 'I don't have a problem with that' or, 'I do it this way and I think everyone should do the same'. Now is the time to help each other and to bear one another's burdens (Galatians 6:2).

Course outline

Title	Key verse	Areas to cover	Media cross-reference
God and your heart	1 John 2:15	Passionate about what?	All
God and your mind	Romans 12:2	Addiction	Music, social networking
God and your eyes	Luke 11:34	What we watch, screens	Video games
God and your words	Colossians 4:6	Things we say, even on MSN and Facebook	MSN, Facebook, texting
God and your hands	Proverbs 6:6	Work and idleness	How media invades our time, temptation to idly surf internet and not be constructive
God and your life	Ephesians 5:8-10	100% of your life belongs to God	The closed bedroom door

LESSON 1

GOD AND YOUR HEART

BIBLE READING

1 John 1:8 – 2:2; 2:15-17
Key verse: Do not love the world or anything in the world. If anyone loves the world, the love of the Father is not in him (1 John 2:15).

TEACHING POINT

Love for God conflicts with love for the world. There is only one number one in your life.

LEADER'S PREPARATION

This session is about raising the awareness amongst the young people of the constant pressure on them to be 'worldly'. The aim is to set up the rest of the series and to introduce the idea of worldliness, which remains a problem and attraction even when we are committed Christians.

'The world' is used in various ways in the Bible. It can mean the physical world, as in Genesis 41:57, 'the famine was severe in all the world', or the people in the world, e.g. John 3:16, 'God so loved the world'. In this passage it means human society in opposition to God.

QUESTIONS

Read 1 John 1:8 – 2:2. We are all sinful, but what does God promise to do? What does Jesus do?

If we confess then God promises to forgive us (1:9). He will purify us (i.e. make us holy). He also provides Jesus as the 'one who speaks in our defence' (2:1). In other words, Jesus speaks up on our behalf. Furthermore, Jesus is the atoning sacrifice – the one who perfectly covers the punishment for our sins.

This opening question is important since the subject passage of this session is dangerous when it is taken out of the context of sin and salvation. A blind obedience to rejecting the world, without the context of this being our response to the rescue God has provided, might lead us into all sorts of legalism and isolation.

Read 1 John 2:15-17. What are we not to do? What are the sort of things that verse 16 defines as worldly?

We are not to love the world – that's simple. (See above for the meaning of 'the world' in this context.) Verse 16 expands on the idea of worldliness. 'The cravings of sinful man' encompass our wrong desires and priorities whatever they may be. 'The lust of his eyes' is about where we look, which is a good indication of our desires and is certainly meant to include sexual lusts. 'The boasting of what he has and does' is about basic materialism and a self-centred world view.

Where do these things come from?

They come from the world, not from God. Worldliness is an attitude that seeks to ignore God and live life our way without him. Think of the lyrics to the song 'My Way', a very popular song at funerals. It is a song that praises a self-centred world and represents that worldly attitude exactly.

What two reasons does John give for not loving the world? (v. 15, 17)

Firstly, it contradicts our love for God (v.15) – *if anyone loves the world, the love of the Father is not in him.* Just as Jesus said, it is impossible to love two masters – you cannot serve the Lord and money (Matthew 6:24).

Secondly, the world is temporary (v.17) – *The world and its desires pass away, but the man who does the will of God lives for ever.* Why put your trust and resources into something that is second best, something that will one day be destroyed?

APPLY:

What sort of things are we tempted to love that are worldly?

As well as possessions and money you may want to steer the discussion towards less materialistic but equally worldly things, e.g. praise from others, status, power and influence, etc.

Are these things permanent or temporary? Why do we crave them?

All worldly things are temporary. The real meat of the question is why we crave them. It might be a sensitive area or even something that the young people have not considered at all, so you might need to take a step back and look at things from a wider perspective, e.g. what do they spend their time and money on, what do they daydream about, what informs decisions such as choice of school subjects, potential careers, etc.?

It is not that there is anything wrong with wanting to do well at school, to be a doctor or spend time with friends. It is our attitude towards these things that matters and this is an indicator of what is going on in our hearts.

Which way is your heart pointing?

Mark 10:17-31 tells the story of a rich young man whose heart was pointing in the wrong direction. Jesus was able quickly to get to the root of his problem – his materialism and status. In doing so Jesus taught some important lessons:

- Our priorities matter as well as what we do with our possessions. Note that Jesus did not ask the rich young man if he had kept the first four commandments (about loving God), only the 'easy', outward looking ones. (v.18-20)
- We cannot do this by ourselves. Changing the way we feel, taking decisions, setting priorities, etc. is not easy. We cannot do it alone. Jesus reminds the disciples that with God all things are possible. (v.27)
- Jesus reminds the disciples how much we have to gain by putting him and his kingdom first. (v.29-30)

Use the story with the group to reflect on the way their hearts are pointing – towards God or towards themselves. Let the reflections lead into a prayer time.

PLANNING THE SESSION

Welcome

- Introduce yourselves.
- Start the meeting with prayer.

Getting to Know You

Play a game that involves describing yourself in three statements based on favourites, e.g. I love X-factor (favourite TV), I like chocolate (favourite food) and I love shopping (favourite hobby). You might want to give people several favourites from which they have to choose three. Have each member of the group write secretly on a card and then mix all the cards up. Then guess who is who from the description, in teams or as a group.

Talk Time

The Bedroom Wall – talk about who you might have had on the bedroom wall (or what groups or football teams, etc they might have followed). Talk about why we move on from following certain groups or doing certain hobbies.

Focus Time

One Hit Wonders quiz – this could be done as a picture quiz, using pictures of past celebrities who are no longer in the public eye, or listening to past musical hits and identifying the artist(s). So many celebrities, groups and songs come and go that we get used to the transient nature of fame.

Bible Time

See the worksheets on pages 68-69 for the Bible Study questions and running order. Photocopy these pages for each group member for use during the study.

Prayer Time

In small groups read and pray about the first commandment (Exodus 20:1-3).

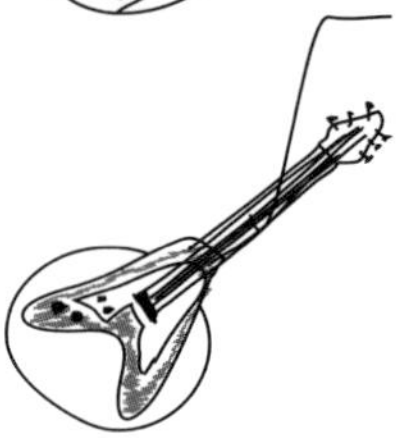

Praise Time

Musical groups – songs such as 'The Lord is gracious and compassionate' (see www.kingswaysongs.com or www.emumusic.com for words and music).

Non-musical groups – read Psalm 25 together.

Extra Ideas

1. If you want further discussion, use the following simple scenario, or make up your own along similar lines. It is based on a real situation, but has been semi-fictionalised and pushed towards an extreme in order to stimulate discussion. You can use the scenario at any point in the session, but it is recommended that you do the Bible study first in order to equip the group to answer profitably.

Permanently Connected

Jason is a technophile, a modern, online young man. He has the latest phone; he is a computer 'geek' in the nicest possible way and can fix anything; he reads pretty much every magazine there is to do with technology. Start a conversation about the latest i-pod and just sit back whilst he gives you every specification in minute detail. He's a very nice person, although sometimes you just have to wonder whether he speaks the same language. The problem comes in the grey areas of the internet, such as downloading music files and movies. Jason knows every trick in the book and is quite happy to distribute his 'free' music to the group.

Is Jason wrong to embrace technology in this way? What are the dangers in his doing this? What does Jason need to consider as a Christian when he is tempted to dabble in the grey areas of downloading and file-sharing? What advice would you give Jason about fitting his faith into his already frantic, modern lifestyle? The group needs to be reminded that file-sharing can be illegal and Christians should obey the law (Romans 13:1).

2. Have the group list their five favourite possessions on a card. Once they have done this tell a story that involves them losing four of these possessions one by one – they have to rip the card up and put it in the bin. The items might be stolen, broken, lost, etc. This forces the group to choose their most treasured possession and introduces the uncomfortable idea of the impermanence of these things.

LESSON 2

GOD AND YOUR MIND

BIBLE READING

Romans 11:32 – 12:2
Key verse: Do not conform any longer to the pattern of this world, but be transformed by the renewing of your mind (Romans 12:2).

TEACHING POINT

A transformed heart leads to a transformed mind. Don't be squeezed by the world any longer.

LEADER'S PREPARATION

The first area of our lives that we are tackling is the mind. We often retreat from the world into our minds, confident that we can behave on the outside and be seen to be authentic Christians, whilst we are really holding back the whole of our thought lives from God. This has disastrous consequences if we let it continue. Our minds need to come under God's control to stop wrong thinking, just as much as our fists need to come under control to stop us hitting other people (hopefully, the latter is not an issue in your group).

QUESTIONS

Read Romans 11:32 – 12:2. Why does Paul begin 12:1 with 'therefore'?

Chapters 1-11 of Romans are an overview of what God has done for us through Jesus. Depending on how well you know Romans you might want to look back through the book and summarise. Otherwise use the doxology at the end of chapter 11 to remind yourselves about how amazing God is and what he has done.

What are we to do in response to God's love and salvation?

Several things are mentioned:

- Offer your bodies as living sacrifices
- Don't conform to the world any longer
- Be transformed by the renewing of your mind.

In other words, we start to act and think differently once we have been saved. It is not that our behaviour will save us (it is a response from us, rather than something we do to curry favour with God), but that we are beginning to change as we grow into the people that God wants us to be.

Why do you think that Paul talks about our minds being transformed? What might he mean?

Transforming our minds means changing our thinking. Outward behaviour takes some willpower, but we can generally control ourselves and be 'good on the outside'. Changing our mindset

is much harder work. It means a re-programming. No longer are we to think as the world thinks, but from now on we take our direction from God (v.2b).

Why are our minds so important that Paul calls for transforming them as the first part of becoming a 'living sacrifice'?

Because without changing our minds any change of behaviour will end in a relapse once any controlling factors (parents, youth leaders, etc.) are no longer around. From the Bible's perspective the change God wants to see in us is not merely a change in outward behaviour, but of the heart (Psalm 51:17). Our hearts and minds are crucial to long-term change in our behaviour (Deuteronomy 30:6).

Apply:

Who is in control of your mind? How will you know if you are still controlling your mind?

A tricky question. Part of the answer is about your thought life. Do you rule your daydreams or does God? Do you choose to think about things that might change your life for your benefit or God's? (e.g. 'this is what I would do if I won a million pounds ...' or 'if I were able to change this part of my life then everything would be better'). Our daydreams show whether we are satisfied or unsatisfied with what God has given us (note that striving for achievement and wanting a good job are not bad things in and of themselves). Perhaps part of bringing our thought life under God's control is learning contentment with where he has placed us – see Philippians 4:11-12.

The other part of the answer is about how we treat our minds. Do we fill them with good things and train them in godliness (through Bible reading and prayer, etc.)? Or do we let

our minds remain unchecked and untrained? If the latter is the case then we will not be free, but we will become 'conformed to the pattern of this world'.

What sort of things do we allow into our minds? How can we filter these things practically?

This is wide-ranging and might produce any number of answers. Music is a classic example of something that is often there in the background these days because of personal stereos. Much discussion has been had in the past about whether or not pop and rock music are appropriate for Christian young people. You will have to judge whether this is the right time to have this discussion.

Nevertheless, the aim of the discussion is to get to the heart of what we feed on visually and aurally. Are we filling our minds with junk or worse, because that will have a detrimental effect on our walk as Christians. The sort of 'filters' we can use include a decision to choose what to watch on television rather than channel surfing, choosing not to listen to music with 'parental guidance' on the cover, using the internet responsibly, etc. The help of parents, friends and older Christians might be necessary to help us with self-discipline.

Consider the following quotation, attributed to Ralph Waldo Emerson:

> Sow a thought and you reap an action;
> sow an action and you reap a habit;
> sow a habit and you reap a character;
> sow a character and you reap a destiny.

How does it describe the descent from mere thoughts to addictive behaviour?

Whilst it is not the Bible, this much quoted idea helps us understand why Paul wants us to train our minds. Our actions are sown in the mind and through actions we grow habits which can be addictive.

What addictions might we need to be careful of, regarding the media that surrounds us the whole time?

Be careful of the discussion that might go on here. It could be an opportunity to raise issues such as pornography, which will be best covered in separate groups for girls and boys (although it is covered again in the next study). It may be that just raising the issue of addiction is a new idea and provokes a good discussion.

A group member may mention something for which they need help. Useful resources are:

CCPAS (Churches Child Protection Advisory Service)
www.ccpas.co.uk

CEOP (Child Exploitation and Online Protection Centre)
www.ceop.police.uk

Childnet International www.childnet-int.org

UKCCIS (UK Council for Child Internet Safety)
www.education.gov.uk/ukccis

PLANNING THE SESSION

Welcome

- Introduce yourselves.
- Start the meeting with prayer.

Getting to Know You

Ask the group to sit in a circle and introduce themselves one by one. However, each person has to have a silly addiction that also begins with the same letter of their name. As you go round in a circle, each person has to introduce all the other people so far and remember their 'addictions' e.g. This is Charles, he is addicted to chocolate; this is Laura, she is addicted to limbo dancing; and I'm Frank, I'm addicted to Frisbee. You could add actions for extra confusion.

Talk Time

Talk about revision (groan!) – there will always be someone revising for a test or exam or something. (Another example might be practising for a driving test). How do they go about doing this? Perhaps aim for ten top tips that the group can come up with together. The point is to identify how the young people are used to using their minds for training themselves. Revision techniques help us with this training. This study is about 'transforming our minds' not to learn maths formulae, but to help us in our battle against worldliness.

Focus Time

On large pieces of paper draw an outline of a person. If you want to do this as a large group, you could make it life-sized. With paint or thick pens draw arrows pointing at the person labelled with things that bombard us day by day and might become addictive or might change us in some other way (i.e. the things that want to 'conform' us – Romans 12:2). Later in the session you could add arrows pushing out of the person labelled with the ways that we resist change and seek to please God.

Bible Time

See the worksheets on pages 70-71 for the Bible Study questions and running order. Photocopy these pages for each group member for use during the study.

Prayer Time

In small groups go over some of the practical ways to help filter what goes into your minds. Pray, asking God to help you control your thought life. Encourage the group to be specific.

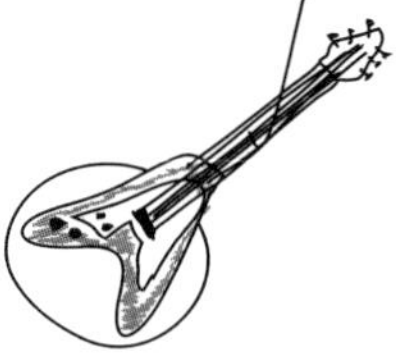

Praise Time

Musical groups – songs such as 'I will offer up my life' (see www.kingswaysongs.com or www.emumusic.com for words and music).

Non-musical groups – read Psalm 32 as an antiphonal reading (two groups reading the verses turn and turn about).

Extra Ideas

1. If you want further discussion, use the following simple scenario, or make up your own along similar lines. It is based on a real situation, but has been semi-fictionalised and pushed towards an extreme in order to stimulate discussion. You can use the scenario at any point in the session, but it is recommended that you do the Bible study first in order to equip the group to answer profitably.

Social Networking

Julie, Jane and Joanne are best friends in real life and on the internet. They are 'friends' on Facebook, follow on Twitter, share photos on Flicker … everything. But one day, as a joke, Julie puts up a picture of Joanne on Facebook with a playful comment that is a little too personal. The trio is beginning to break up and Jane is caught between the other two and her friendship is getting used as a bargaining tool.

What would you say to the three girls – together or individually? To what extent do you think our 'online' relationships interfere with or spoil *real* friendships?

2. If you choose to talk about music in particular, you might want to have a session where several of the young people play a favourite song and explain why they like it.

LESSON 3

GOD AND YOUR EYES

BIBLE READING

Luke 11:29-36.

Key verse: Your eye is the lamp of your body. When your eyes are good, your whole body also is full of light. But when they are bad, your body also is full of darkness (Luke 11:34).

TEACHING POINT

A transformed heart leads to healthy eyes. Let in the light of Jesus' teaching to counter the darkness of the world.

LEADER'S PREPARATION

'Be careful little eyes what you see' is the way an age-old children's song goes. After our hearts and minds, our eyes are probably one of the hardest things to bring under God's control. We are bombarded daily with images. That's our world. These images can be innocuous or juvenile or sexually provocative and all are either in our faces on billboards or just one click away on the internet.

The eye could be the lamp of the body in the sense that it enables the body to find its way. Your eye must be good in order for it to direct 'your whole body' (semitic expression meaning you, yourself) towards what is good.

Alternatively, it could mean that the whole body (person) is viewed as a room or a house. The purpose of the eye is to illuminate this room, to ensure that it is 'full of light'. The eye serves as a window in a windowless room. Therefore, to be full of light, the eye must be good. If the eye is bad (glass caked with soot, wick untrimmed, fuel depleted, etc.) the person remains in darkness.

The 'good' eye is the one fixed on God. The result is to be 'full of light', i.e. to understand divine truth and exhibit pure behaviour. This lifestyle acts as a witness and sheds light all around (v.33).

QUESTIONS

Read Luke 11:29-32. To whom is Jesus likening himself? What was the original response from the Ninevites in particular?

Jesus likens himself to Solomon receiving the Queen of Sheba (1 Kings 10) and Jonah preaching to Nineveh (Jonah 3). The Ninevites repented at the preaching of Jonah, that is why they will condemn 'this generation' (i.e. the Jews in Jesus' time). They heeded Jonah's warnings, but the current generation are ignoring Jesus, who is greater than Jonah.

This context is important, because it gets us thinking about the next passage and the question of what to do with Jesus' teaching when we hear it.

Read Luke 11:33-36. Jesus describes his teaching as a lamp. What should happen to a lamp and why? How should we treat Jesus' teaching?

Jesus' teaching is the light that must not be hidden. It is there to be listened to and obeyed. (N.B. Jesus' teaching doesn't just mean what we read in the gospels. Since all Scripture is inspired by God (2 Timothy 3:16) and Jesus is God's ultimate Word (John 1:1-2) we can reasonably say that the whole Bible is Jesus' teaching.)

Lamps should be displayed in a prominent place to provide a wide coverage of light. So Jesus' teaching should not be hidden away, but on display. It is there to throw light onto our situations, not to be smothered by other things.

Maybe think about the ways that we might try to put Jesus' teaching 'under a bowl'. For example, in the way we might limit our study of the Bible to Sundays; to be academic about it and not relate it to real life; or to apply it to other people but not to ourselves (e.g. 'so and so really needs to hear this lesson about gossip because they are always talking about other people').

What might Jesus mean when he says that the eye is the lamp of the body, in the context of talking about how we treat his teaching?

This is a complicated metaphor (see Leader's Preparation) but it helps to continue to think of Jesus' teaching as the light. Our eyes are responsible for what goes into our body (v.34). We can either be looking at the light of Jesus' teaching and taking it in, or we can be avoiding it – taking in darkness. The more we seek to obey Jesus, follow his teaching and fill our bodies with light, the less darkness there will be in us. If our eyes are bad, then we will fill up with darkness.

Jesus says, 'See to it, then, that the light within you is not darkness' (v.35). He means that the things we take in with our eyes should be good and edifying things, not sinful things contrary to what Jesus teaches.

Apply:
How might knowing our Bibles really well help us when we face the temptation of looking at the wrong sorts of material?

The more we know scripture the more we will be able to fight off temptations to look in the wrong places. There are many Bible verses that might help us (e.g. lads could put Job 31:1 on a post-it note on their computers). In a similar way to the topic about the mind, if we are training our eyes to look at good things we will be squeezing out the darkness. One of the reasons for a daily quiet time is to be constantly reminded of Jesus' teaching and not to leave room for other things.

You may want to talk about how to get into the habit of reading the Bible daily without being legalistic about it and different ways that Bible reading can be kept fresh.

What practical ways can you think of to help each other live a Christian life in a society so full of visual images, many of which are unhelpful?

We can't walk around with our eyes on the pavement the whole time, but we live in a society where even billboards can be fairly 'fleshy'. The group may well come up with some really good ideas to help one another. Here are two or three to get started:

- *What do you do with the second look?* We are bombarded with visual images so much that it is hard not to see things. However, whilst we might not be able to help seeing things at first glance, we are totally responsible for what we do with the second look. This applies to billboards as well as to the channels that we might glimpse when we are channel hopping late at night. (Should Christians, especially lads, train themselves not to get into the habit of watching late night telly alone?)

- Using scripture to help us. One verse has already been mentioned above. Can we think of others and helpful places to put them? For example, one leader has had Hebrews 12:1-3 on a piece of paper in the front of his filo-fax for years in an effort to help himself 'run the race' and not get entangled. Try these helpful verses too – Proverbs 6:16-19, something from Proverbs 7 e.g. v.25, Psalm 51:10, Ephesians 4:1, Colossians 3:1-2, and many others).

- Learn to mock. Advertisers use visual images to attract us. It works because we always think that the grass is greener elsewhere and that we are entitled to whatever image of paradise is being depicted, whether it is a foreign holiday or a new kitchen. As Christians we must learn to see through this stuff and be content with what God has given us (1 Tim 6:6ff). It doesn't mean that holidays, new kitchens or even underwear is sinful, although perhaps the way the latter is advertised is wrong. We are not all called to lives of monastic poverty. We need to see everything – TV adverts, billboards, reality television and the national lottery – for what it really is, the peddling of a world that rejects God's good blueprint for life and tries to impose a glamorous but fake blueprint of its own. Talk about how you might train yourselves to apply a godly understanding to the programmes you watch on television.

The internet. Never before have people had such a powerful visual tool at their disposal. What are the particular dangers for Christians in all this visual content?

This question speaks for itself and may lead to a discussion about pornography in particular. This might necessitate a discussion in single sex groups. You will find that more of the boys than you think will regularly look at things they shouldn't.

However, don't let the issue of pornography take over. There are many other issues with the internet that are worth discussing, e.g. when to post pictures of yourselves or your friends, how to be responsible for online picture albums, getting distracted by the pop-up adverts, etc. How we behave on social networking sites like Facebook and internet messaging sites is covered in a future session.

It is important that our young people know how to use the internet safely. UKCCIS has developed the 'Click Clever, Click Safe Code' (see page 30 for website details).

When using Facebook the group members need to be aware of the following:

- The default privacy setting is set to public sharing of information, so they may be sharing more than they want to. They can adjust the settings to limit who has access to personal information.
- Once something is posted, anyone who sees it can copy it and post it elsewhere.
- Any concerns they have whilst online should be reported, e.g. via the 'Click CEOP Safety' button (see page 30 for website details).

PLANNING THE SESSION

Welcome

- Introduce yourselves.
- Start the meeting with prayer.

Getting to Know You

Since this session is about visual images you could start with the classic baby photo quiz – either of the leaders or, if you are organised, the whole group. Alternatively you could ask people to bring a favourite holiday picture and explain why they like it. (Again, prior organisation means you might be able to do this as a Powerpoint show.)

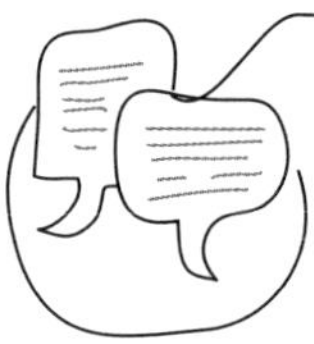

Talk Time

We are so accustomed to having visual images that we take them for granted. You could talk about striking adverts that are on the television currently, exploring why they work and why they are memorable. If you have time you could try to reproduce the advert without visuals, i.e. just by speaking, not even using gestures. This calls for a bit of dramatic invention.

Focus Time

Play a game that involves describing something for others to deduce what it is. In a game called 'Architect's Nightmare' half the group have a bunch of lego pieces whilst the rest have a completed model behind a screen. The half with the model have to describe it so that the others can reproduce it. Any other game emphasising the importance of visual images would work as well.

Bible Time

See the worksheets on pages 72-73 for the Bible Study questions and running order. Photocopy these pages for each group member for use during the study.

Prayer Time

In small groups go over the practical ways you can help each other live a Christian life in a world full of visual images, many of which are unhelpful. Pray, asking God to help you control what you look at in the coming week.

Praise Time

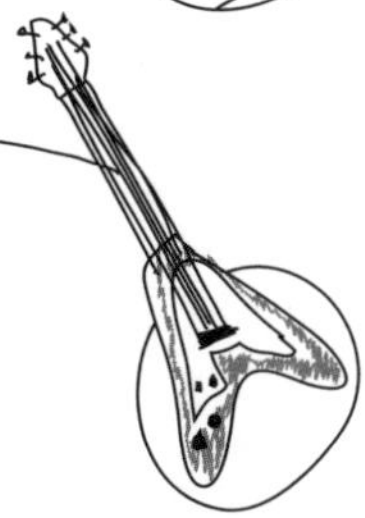

Musical groups – songs such as 'Our God reigns' (see www. kingswaysongs.com or www.emumusic.com for words and music).

Non-musical groups – read Psalm 19 together.

Extra Ideas

1. If you want further discussion, use the following simple scenario, or make up your own along similar lines. It is based on a real situation, but has been semi-fictionalised and pushed towards an extreme in order to stimulate discussion. You can use the scenario at any point in the session, but it is recommended that you do the Bible study first in order to equip the group to answer profitably.

Video Games

Gaz has a difficult life. He finds it difficult to fit in and gets picked on a bit at school, so he spends a lot of time playing computer games. He is not addicted, but he does like the release of charging into a virtual building and firing off a spray of virtual bullets. The trouble is that his parents notice that he has started to get into fights at school. Physical action has begun to be the first port of call rather than sorting out differences verbally. The link between violence and video games is a matter of debate, of course, but the worry for Gaz's parents and teachers is that he enjoys the violence so much. His parents turn to the youth group leader for help.

What advice do you have for Gaz and his parents? How might the youth group leader respond to the request for help?

It is important that the group recognises that Gaz is being bullied, which is unacceptable. For help with bullying issues go to www.beatbullying.org.

2. As an extra activity you could play a game that involves matching advertisements to their tag lines, or taking old adverts to see if the young people can identify the product. Alternatively, to show how visual images get lodged in our minds, have the group try to identify some famous world landmarks from their silhouettes. Make it as easy or as hard as you like.

LESSON 4

GOD AND YOUR WORDS

BIBLE READING

Colossians 4:2-6, Ephesians 4:25-29; 5:4.
Key verse: Let your conversation be always full of grace, seasoned with salt, so that you may know how to answer everyone (Colossians 4:6).

TEACHING POINT

A transformed heart leads to speech full of grace. Spice your conversation with the salt of the gospel.

LEADER'S PREPARATION

This is possibly the 'biggie'. Everyone knows that you shouldn't look at indecent images on the net, but who's to say how you should behave in a chatroom or on instant messaging sites or Facebook or … you get the picture. There will probably be more opinion, more discussion and possibly more resentment about being told how to behave on social networking sites than anything else. As Christian youth leaders we cannot lay down the law about such things without it leading to a pious and legalistic youth group. That is why the key verse is a positive one – do make your conversation gospel centred and full of grace. The negative verse which prohibits foul language is Ephesians 4:29. It is just as important, but doesn't reach far enough.

As with all of our behaviour, we are encouraging the young people to look into their hearts to see how the transformation there will affect their speech, both verbal and written on computers/phones. Saved hearts are transformed hearts. Transformed hearts will strive to obey Christ out of thankfulness and a desire to grow in Christian stature. That even affects Facebook!

QUESTIONS

Read Colossians 4:2-6. For what is Paul asking prayer? What sort of proclamation is Paul emphasising?

Paul is emphasising gospel proclamation. This is what he asks prayer for (v.3-4). Paul, the great evangelist, never stops looking for opportunities to preach the gospel and calls on the Colossians to pray for him as he evangelises ('open a door'). 'Devote yourselves' (v.2) implies perseverance. 'The mystery of Christ' is the gospel (see 1:25-26).

How should we present ourselves to others? What does this mean in practice?

We should be wise in the way we act (v.5) and our conversation should always be full of grace and seasoned with salt (v.6). In the Bible Jesus is the wisest person and the representation of God's wisdom. To be truly wise is to be godly and Christ-like. Paul is calling for wise actions from Christians as they meet those outside the church. He is also calling for conversation full of the grace of God. God's grace gives us what we don't deserve, so our conversation needs to be godly, conducted in such a way that we see people as God sees them (that is, not as we see them, e.g. 'They're not worth talking to' or 'They always insult me, so I give as good as I get!').

All this is 'seasoned with salt'. Salt is a preservative and adds taste. Similarly the Christian's conversation is to be good and wholesome, adding the gospel into our conversation wherever we can to give the conversation context. Not that every conversation has to be deep and meaningful; those conversations about the weather are okay. But if all we do is talk about trivial stuff, especially with our best friends, then we have missed a trick. We are to make the most of every opportunity (v.5). There is no off-switch for evangelism, says Paul, and no day off.

When Paul says 'so that you may know how to answer everyone' (v.6) he means that we should be ready to defend our beliefs and challenge others, asking and answering tricky questions (see 1 Peter 3:15-16) and never to give up an opportunity.

Read Ephesians 4:25-29; 5:4. Make 2 lists of the sort of talk Paul is condemning and what he is encouraging. Discuss which things on the list are difficult to stop or start and which are easy.

You may want to do the list in small groups or as a large group on flip-chart paper. Some of the items are straightforward, e.g. truthfulness versus falsehood. Others are harder to pin down, e.g. what exactly is 'unwholesome'? There should be lots to talk about. Try to avoid drawing lines in the sand about what words are allowed and what are not. What is important is not legalistic rules but a heart that is turned towards God and seeks to please him. If we ask the question, 'how can I serve God well in this

conversation?' The answer about what we should and shouldn't say will become obvious.

N.B. you might get a question about grieving the Holy Spirit (v.30), a confusing phrase. It is simplest to say that he is the Holy Spirit so he is grieved by unholiness; he is the Spirit of truth, so he is grieved by untruthfulness. Notice that the word 'sealed' refers back to Ephesians 1:13 – the seal being a mark of ownership. Because we belong to him, God has given us and all Christians his Holy Spirit as a mark of acceptance.

Apply:

Are there any conversations that you should not take part in? Are you ready for the consequences of being different in the way you speak?

This is sensitive. No young person likes to be different. Staying quiet is an option, of course, but that is passive. Only the very bold and outgoing will be able to sway conversations, so look out for the quieter members of the group and look for ways to encourage them. For example, we don't all have to be the life and soul of the party. Perhaps they are quiet and mainly chat to only one or two people. How does being a Christian affect those relationships?

What about online chat? Should the same rules apply? How should we speak to people through texts and messaging when we can't see them or, worse still, when they are not even present online?

If you thought you were getting through the material quickly, then this is when the session will begin to hot up. There will be many different opinions and probably many different ideas of what should and shouldn't be done. However, the aim is really to steer the young people towards thinking more about their witness as Christians over the internet. Conversation doesn't stop at face to face chats; it is everywhere these days.

What behaviour do you need to change regarding your online or text conversations? What practical ways can you think of together that will help them to be full of grace and seasoned with salt?

This question is not about the rights and wrongs of using social networking or instant messaging sites, but instead is about practical ideas for change. Some people use Bible texts at the bottom of their blog pages. Others use twitter and Facebook to 'announce' great things that are happening in their lives spiritually.

A great example of a Christian Blog run by a young man (well, youngish these days) is: www.hughbourne.co.uk – aka the Ramblings of Hughbo. It has won the 'Young Christian Blogger of the Year' twice in succession.

Many of the group will have mobiles that allow them to take and send photos attached to e-mails. 'Sexting' is when they take nude or suggestive photos of themselves and send them to a boyfriend or girlfriend. This can have unintended, disastrous consequences. 'Exposed' is a good video demonstrating this and can be found on www.thinkuknow.co.uk. Sexting is also illegal if the person being photographed is under 18. Advice can be sought from either CCPAS or CEOP (see page 30 for website details).

PLANNING THE SESSION

Welcome

- Introduce yourselves.
- Start the meeting with prayer.

Getting to Know You

This session is about speech, so ask for volunteers to speak for 1 minute on a subject without hesitation, repetition or deviation – prizes for anyone who can. If you don't want to play that, play another speaking game like, In One Word or Taboo.

Talk Time

Who do you talk to? Some people will talk to lots of people, others are shy. Can you each come up with a spider diagram (or something similar) of the conversations you might have on a typical school day. Hopefully the interconnections will be amazing. We really talk to more people than we probably give ourselves credit for. Just imagine if each one of those conversations spread a little more 'salt' of the gospel. (See the study for what that means).

Focus Time

The key verse for this study calls for wisdom in the way we speak to others. The aim of the study is to apply this to our conversations and how we interact on the internet. Draw up a list of wise and foolish things that people might have done. This can be light-hearted if you want or serious (but you have to be careful about what people might share). For an added twist have people draw a picture of what they might have done, if that is appropriate, and let the others guess.

Bible Time

See the worksheets on pages 74-75 for the Bible Study questions and running order. Photocopy these pages for each group member for use during the study.

Prayer Time

Pray in small groups, asking God for help in controlling your tongue.

Praise Time

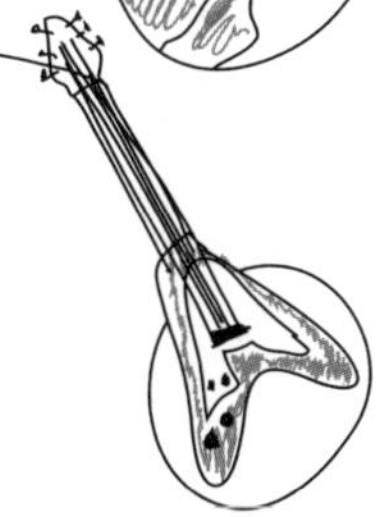

Musical groups – general praise songs (see www. kingswaysongs com or www.emumusic.com for words and music).

Non-musical groups – read Psalm 34 together.

Extra Ideas

1. If you want further discussion, use the following simple scenario, or make up your own along similar lines. It is based on a real situation, but has been semi-fictionalised and pushed towards an extreme in order to stimulate discussion. You can use the scenario at any point in the session, but it is recommended that you do the Bible study first in order to equip the group to answer profitably.

Virtual words don't hurt?

Jenny and Cameron go to the same youth group and have grown up together. They go to different schools but see each other most days. They are not going out. The group are all active on MSN (or similar) and know that Jenny and Cameron often chat via the internet, often late at night. Jenny sometimes says unkind things about Cameron on Facebook to other members of the group 'as a joke' but keeps insisting they chat online every night. After a few months the 'jokes' start to creep into conversations when the youth group are actually together.

What advice would you give the other members of the group? How would you approach Jenny and what would you say to her?

2. How difficult is it to control our tongues? Play the Yes/No game with the group. Taking turns ask the members of the groups questions that require a Yes/No answer. Their challenge is to go for thirty seconds without saying Yes/No. Conclusion – it is not as easy as it seems.

LESSON 5

GOD AND YOUR HANDS

BIBLE READING

Proverbs 6:6-11.

Go to the ant, you sluggard; consider its ways and be wise! (Proverbs 6:6)

TEACHING POINT

A transformed heart leads to working hands. Don't be a screen junkie.

LEADER'S PREPARATION

I like the word 'sluggard', it's a word we don't use very often these days, which is our loss. It also reminds me of certain people (and myself at times!). Our society is one in which leisure time is highly valued, but this has only been a realistic concept for most people for less than half a century. The amount of leisure time you have and what you are able to do with it are strong indicators of social status. We forget that the majority of the world's population have to work hard for a living, or live at subsistence level. We are privileged.

The internet invades both our work and leisure time like almost nothing else and, probably, in a way that television did in the 50s and 60s. But since the internet is not mentioned in the Bible the questions are: what level should Christians set for online time? How responsible should we be in our work time (yes, that includes schoolwork!) about timekeeping? Should we let ourselves get 'hooked' on time consuming online activities that eat up vast amounts of leisure time too? For example, online games (Massive Multiplier Online Roleplaying Games and others), chat rooms and social networks or just YouTube. Note that some of these questions might apply to television for some people, but it doesn't seem to be in the same league as the internet at just eating up the hours.

This study aims to raise some of these questions for discussion by starting with what the Bible has to say about work. Be prepared for a little bit of a 'paper chase', because the theme of work and rest is quite a big one in the Bible. If you want to pare down the study because of time restraints, stick to the questions about the key verses of Proverbs 6:6-11.

QUESTIONS

Read Proverbs 6:6-11. What is it about the ant that lazy people need to consider? (v.6-8)

The ant is organised and hard-working. We all know this from nature programmes, but remember that Proverbs was written by arguably the world's first biologist (1 Kings 4:33-34). Even without bosses to tell them what to do the ants gather food at the right time and store it. Solomon uses the Proverbs 'key word' – wisdom. It is undoubtedly wise to store food at harvest for the winter time, but in Proverbs 'wisdom' also points us to living life God's way and with his wisdom.

What temptation is faced by the sluggard? (v.9-10)

The basic problem is that he is too comfortable – the duvet is too warm, the pillow too soft and getting up is too much effort. Talk with the group about whether they can relate to this. When do they find it easy to get up and when is it difficult? Verse 10 is how the Bible expresses that phrase that is heard in most houses: 'Just five more minutes, pleeeeeease!' Inertia – the reluctance of something to move – is a common phenomenon amongst us all.

What are the consequences of behaving like a sluggard? (v.11)

Poverty and scarcity will creep up on you and it will seem like a surprise. The metaphor is that they will mug you. Before you realise it, your inaction and laziness will catch up. You'll run out of money and you'll run out of food. Using the idea of bandits and armed men emphasises that this will not be a pleasant experience.

Apply:

Read Proverbs 12:11. How might 'chasing fantasies' be a trap we might fall into on the internet?

This question is designed to introduce the idea of the internet often causing us to waste time. We do seem to switch off to time and common sense when we are online, not just in the things we might say in ill-judged e-mails, but also in the sites we visit just because there is a link. Ask the group whether they think that good judgment can be lost 'online'.

Work, Rest and Play in the Bible

Read Genesis 2:15. What is Adam to do in the Garden of Eden? Is this a surprise?

God puts Adam to work (also hinted at in 1:28). Genesis 2:8-14 describe a literal paradise – it sounds like a great place to live. And yet the surprise is that there is still work to be done. Work is not one of the effects of the Fall – we are created to work for God as his under-rulers, looking after his good creation. Only after Adam and Eve's disobedience does work become a chore (Genesis 3:17-19) as the relationship between mankind and the environment becomes spoilt. (Note that there are many broken relationships as a result of the Fall – between man and God; men and women; people and the environment). Even the punishment of exile from Eden includes the idea of hard work (3:23). Like so many things, work began as a good part of God's design, but became twisted into something we resent.

Read Exodus 20:8-10. Why do you think that the people needed reminding about God's rest after creation?

God is a God of rest. If you look at the pattern in Genesis 1 and 2 there does not seem to be a conclusion to day 7. For all the other days the pattern reads, 'there was evening and there was morning – the 1st ... 6th day'. But day 7 doesn't seem to end. Once God's work of creation was done, he rested. Through the 4th commandment God reminds his people of his rest. He does it by giving them a day off (remember, they weren't to collect manna on the 7th day) and blessing it. Genesis 2 and Exodus 20 together tell us that the Sabbath points us forward, not back. We don't rest from work just because we look back to the 7th day of creation, but because we look forward to a heavenly rest (see Hebrews 4:8-11). Incidentally, God does not rest from his sustaining work (Hebrews 1:3) and he works in the lives of people (Psalm 103:6).

Apply:

Read Colossians 3:22-24. What are 'slaves' (workers) told to do and why?

Slaves are to work with all their heart. Remember, not all slaves were chained to an oar, many were household or civil servants. Slaves are to do this as if they are working for the Lord and not men. Talk about how this might affect the way we prioritise and use our time.

What other reasons do we have for working hard? (1 Thessalonians 4:11-12)

Paul recognises that living the Christian life is going to be hard. It might mean standing out from the crowd in the way that we work (and this means more than academic work, of course). To be diligent, honest and hard-working is a huge challenge in a world full of people who do the least they can get away with and who are often dishonest about how they spend their time. Paul gives two reasons for behaving like this – to win respect (for the gospel) and not to be a burden on others.

How might you need to change the way you think about work? What challenge do you face regarding the way you spend time on the internet?

These two questions need to be thought about in advance so that you can guide a meaningful discussion.

PLANNING THE SESSION

Welcome

- Introduce yourselves.
- Start the meeting with prayer.

Getting to Know You

This session is about how we spend our time. As an opening activity get the young people to draw some pie charts, either individually or in groups, about how they spend their time, either during a day or a week. Be as honest and accurate as you can. You could prepare your own chart as an example. You could set the target of keeping a time chart for a week. Make sure they include time spent on the internet.

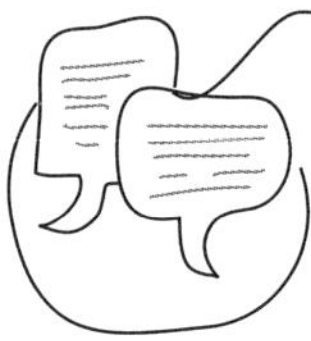

Talk Time

Talk about the charts generated in the first activity. Are there any surprises? What do people spend the most time doing outside of school? Lead this discussion towards the subject of time spent on the internet, how that time is spent and how easy it is to get hooked just surfing without actually achieving anything.

Focus Time

The focus is on work and idleness. If the groups like acting, play charades with the answers all based on different jobs. Alternatively, give the group jobs to do, e.g. a litter pick around the building, vacuuming the floor, washing up the coffee mugs. Don't spend too long doing this (you might want to make it the only opening activity). When you reconvene talk about the purpose and value of the jobs they have done. Talk about why work is such an important part of the human experience.

Bible Time

See the worksheets on pages 76-77 for the Bible Study questions and running order. Photocopy these pages for each group member for use during the study.

Prayer Time

In small groups, thank God for his good gift of work and ask him to help you use your time wisely.

Praise Time

Musical groups – songs such as 'All my days' (see www kingswaysongs.com or www.emumusic.com for words and music).

Non-musical groups – read Psalm 145 together.

Extra Ideas

1. If you want further discussion, use the following simple scenario, or make up your own along similar lines. It is based on a real situation, but has been semi-fictionalised and pushed towards an extreme in order to stimulate discussion. You can use the scenario at any point in the session, but it is recommended that you do the Bible study first in order to equip the group to answer profitably.

Idleness

Simon loves his Playstation and plays on it every moment that he can. His conversations with his family are somewhat monosyllabic, but they think this is fairly normal for teenage boys! Simon's friends see another side to him, however. He is withdrawn and doesn't go out much. He is tired because he stays up late. The console seems to be taking over his life and turning him into somebody else.

What do you think the friends should do? What advice would you give Simon's parents?

2. Find out from one of the many websites that deal in useless information and silly facts about how we spend our time, e.g. how long we spend brushing our teeth in our whole life time or how long we spend on the loo each year (about 2½ days!) Then run a quiz based on this information.

3. There is a book around at the moment (The Winter of our Disconnect, by Sarah Maushart) written by a Mom (she's American) who 'unplugged' her whole family for six months – no TV, no internet, no mobiles, nothing. The results were a revival of interest in other pursuits, such as music and reading. Why not challenge the whole group to live without screens for a week? You could be as strict (deny everything) or as easygoing (just no internet) as you like. Give everyone a challenge to fill the time with something new, such as a book to read, jogging, or a craft-based hobby. After a week report back on the experience.

LESSON 6

GOD AND YOUR LIFE

BIBLE READING

Ephesians 5:1-16.
Key verse: Live as children of light (for the fruit of the light consists in all goodness, righteousness and truth) and find out what pleases the Lord (Ephesians 5:8-10).

TEACHING POINT

A transformed heart leads to a changed life. Don't compartmentalise your life.

LEADER'S PREPARATION

We are all good at compartmentalising our lives, not just the people who are organised. We all put certain partitions up between the different areas of life. School stays separate from family; family from friends; friends from other friends. However, we are all often guilty of trying to separate God from all of these other things and trying to contain him in his own 'box'.

The aim of this study is to try to think 'outside the box' – to stop trying to put God in a box and to give back to him control over our whole lives. For the Christian, it is artificial to think of God being just a part of our lives, or Christianity as just one of many interests we might have. When we become Christians we do not add one more box to the many that make up our lives; rather, there is now one big box in which to put all the others.

From the perspective of these studies which focus on the media, this final session is concerned with the way that we might assume that, because we are essentially 'alone' on the internet and we are very often physically alone in the room or the house, we can hide away our use (and abuse) of the internet in its own little box. This is not the case, of course. If we think this way we have reckoned without an omniscient God who sees all that we do.

The purpose, however, is not to scare people into behaving well – that will just instil a form of legalism into the young people. Instead, by appealing to the heart and relying on God's grace, this session seeks to encourage the young people to live their lives one hundred per cent for God and turn to him in repentance when they fail to do so.

Ephesians 5 will help us see how God's people are to live in the light. Now that we are saved it is our aim to live for the God who saved us. Paul has explained to the Ephesians how they are saved in chapters 1-3. Our study lies in the middle of chapters 4-6, all about our personal response and Christian lifestyle. Chapter 4:1 gives an overarching phrase that guides us through the final three chapters.

QUESTIONS

Read Ephesians 5:1-2. As Christians, what is our new status with God?

We are his 'dearly loved children'. We know how much we are loved because of the enormous sacrifice Christ made on our behalf (verse 2). At the beginning of the study it is worth spending a moment to think about both these things. Reflect on how big the price of our salvation was and how we are now adopted into God's family. There will be some pretty strict dos and don'ts in the rest of the passage and we must remember the context of God's great love for us. The guidelines on how to live are not the unpredictable whims of a vindictive God; but the desire of a loving God to see his creation living back in harmony with himself.

Read Ephesians 5:3-16. What were we once and what are we now? (v.8)

We were once darkness and now we are light. Paul uses this 'transformation' idea elsewhere in this book. If you have got time compare this verse with 2:1-5 and 2:19-20. Note also that Paul does not say that we were 'in' darkness, but that we *were* darkness – the darkness of sin, where there is no light of Christ. Now we are 'light in the Lord' – we have become light, which chases out darkness. It is much easier for light to encroach into darkness, because darkness cannot consume the light, it happens the other way around. And that is what is happening now in our lives, says Paul.

Use the following table to note down the attributes of light and darkness. (v.9-14)

Light	Darkness
Fruitful: goodness, righteousness and truth (v.9)	Fruitless (v.11)
Pleasing to God (v.10)	Shameful (v.12)
Exposing, making visible (v.13)	Secret (v.12)

Use the table or big bits of paper for this question. The purpose is to become familiar with the passage and to identify how light and darkness contrast. Remember this is a metaphor for our deeds.

How does Paul contrast our lives now with what they once were? (v.15-16)

We now live lives that are wise, meaning Christ-like (Christ is our example to follow and the archetype of wisdom). This means we have to take care how we live (v.15); not because to sin is to fail – we are not yet in heaven and sin is still a reality in our lives – but because we *are* light we must take care to live as the light. We will need to still say sorry and receive forgiveness for the times we mess up.

'Making the most of every opportunity' could mean a number of things. It could certainly refer to not missing chances to witness and talk with others about the gospel. There is all the more reason to do this since 'the days are evil'. However, it could also apply to our general time management. It is very easy to fritter away time (particularly on games consoles and the internet) when time is so very precious and the days we live in so evil. We need to 'purposely engage in buying (our time) back from the mere use of self if our life is going to amount to anything' as Kent Hughes puts it. This hints at determination and purpose as we get up in the morning, not drifting through life.

God owns our lives. He is our commanding officer, as Paul puts it in 2 Timothy 2:4. If we are to serve him properly, it is with all of our lives. Explore the three images of service in 2 Timothy 2 if you have time – the soldier, the athlete and the farmer. Ask in what ways each has to work hard, and what reward they are working for. How do these ideas apply to the lives of the young people in the group?

Apply:

Think about some of the attributes of 'Light'. What might these mean for us and our lives?

Don't spend too long on this question – it is an introduction to the application questions. However, do talk about the attributes listed in the table above and about what 'pleasing to God' might mean. The deeds of the light are 'visible' because they are in the light. You could talk about what this means when we are alone physically, but still in view of God and 'in step' with the Spirit (Galatians 5:25).

Read Ephesians 5:3-7. What are the implications for us as we try to put the above things into action? What do you think 'not even a hint' means?

Paul often makes lists like this (e.g. Colossians 3:3-11) and packs a lot of prohibitions into a very small space. We are not meant to treat these lists as merely a checklist, so that when we have ticked everything off we can sit back and relax. For Paul these lists are summaries of a particular character or lifestyle. There will naturally be areas in which we struggle more than others, but our aim is 'not even a hint'. That phrase means that it is not just in our own minds that we must be clear about these things – we must not even give anyone the opportunity to think that we might have sinned – it is about appearances. This might lead to a discussion about the way others perceive us, what they tacitly assume we do, or about whether being passive (i.e. not saying anything) leads to the assumption that we are like everyone else.

Note: verse 5 could be a bit of a sticking point. We all sin and therefore we are all impure. Does this mean that it is impossible to gain the inheritance (heaven)? The answer is yes and no. We cannot achieve it by ourselves, we need God's help. But Paul has already explained what God has done for us in the first half of Ephesians. Read through Ephesians 1–3 (or 2:1-10 if there are time constraints) to explore what the gospel really is. There may be group members who need to hear this good news. Once we have received the gospel the answer is most emphatically 'yes', we can gain the inheritance, it is guaranteed (see Ephesians 1:13-14). Our calling as Christians is to 'live a life worthy', meaning more than just 'do the best you can'. We are to throw our heart and soul, all our energy into this new lifestyle, which is ours through the grace of God.

What changes might you need to make to your lifestyle to ensure that every compartment belongs to God and that you obey him, even when there is no one else around?

The answers to this practical question will be different for each member of the group, but there may be some broad principles. Accountability is a good place to start. Challenge the group on whether they have one good Christian friend who has permission to ask the awkward questions ranging from 'when did you last have a quiet time?' to 'what were you watching on the internet at midnight last night when I saw you were also on MSN?'

It might be worth spending some time discussing the unwisdom of making close friendships with those whose lifestyles are described in verses 3-5.

PLANNING THE SESSION

Welcome

- Introduce yourselves.
- Start the meeting with prayer.

Getting to Know You

This session is all about our whole lives. There will be many things that the group members don't know about each other. Play two truths and a lie, where each member of the group makes three statements about themselves and everyone tries to guess the false statement. The idea is to let people into new areas of our lives that we might have kept separate from the youth group previously.

Talk Time

Talk about the concept of 'Big Brother' – the idea that everything you do is on display all the time. You could even show a clip from The Truman Show or EdTV (choose clips from the latter carefully). What would it feel like? Would the young people like to live a life like Truman's? Why do we like to have our privacy? The aim of the discussion is to get across the idea that we all like to have our own space and, sometimes, we even imagine that God doesn't care what we do with 'our time'.

Focus Time

Collect lots of boxes (or use paper if you don't have boxes). Ask the young people to write down different aspects of their lives on different boxes – you may have to do this as a group. School could be on one box, friends on another; shopping, family and relaxing could be on other boxes. Ask where their Christian faith fits into this series of boxes or paper. Then reveal a very large box that was previously hidden. Put all the boxes with different aspects of our lives inside the big one labelled God. Talk about whether the group members compartmentalise their lives and try to fit God into his little place away from some of the precious aspects of life that are 'ours'.

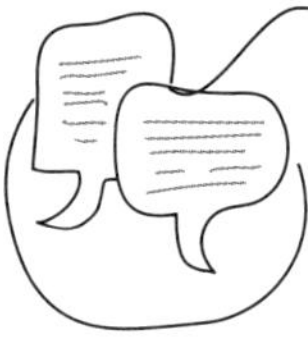

Bible Time

See the worksheets on pages 78-79 for the Bible Study questions and running order. Photocopy these pages for each group member for use during the study.

Prayer Time

In small groups, talk about areas of your life that you have not surrendered to God's control. Pray, thanking God for his gift of forgiveness and asking him to help you live a life that is pleasing to him.

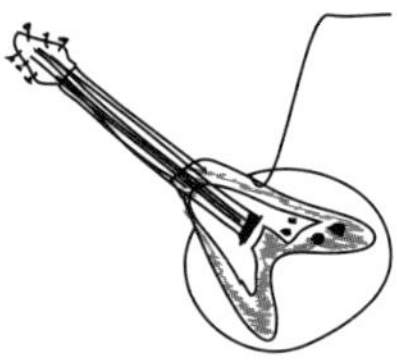

Praise Time

Musical groups – songs such as 'All my days' and 'Our God reigns' (see www.kingswaysongs.com or www.emumusic.com for words and music).

Non-musical groups – read Psalm 96 together.

Extra Ideas

1. If you want further discussion, use the following simple scenario, or make up your own along similar lines. It is based on a real situation, but has been semi-fictionalised and pushed towards an extreme in order to stimulate discussion. You can use the scenario at any point in the session, but it is recommended that you do the Bible study first in order to equip the group to answer profitably.

Home Alone

Nick is in the sixth form with a lot of study time. He doesn't have to be in college all the time and is often home during the day when his parents are out. His parents have given him free use of the computer and there don't seem to be any checks other than a firewall. Nick is a committed Christian and his parents trust him with the internet. The truth is that Nick is not looking at anything he shouldn't, but his friends all assume that he does and make suggestive comments when he gets off the bus. Nick says nothing, but one Sunday he shares this with the rest of the youth group because he has had enough of the teasing. What advice would you give him?

2. Sometimes older teenagers like the irony of doing crafts aimed at younger children. If you think your group might respond to the challenge, try making 'shadow profiles' of members of the group. Stick a piece of white paper to the wall and use a very bright light (like an OHP) to get a crisp shadow of someone in profile. Draw around it carefully and then cut the image out. This should then be mounted on a black piece of paper. You could add a sticker with a verse from Ephesians 5, e.g. vv.9-10 'Live as children of the light and find out what pleases the Lord'.

GOD AND YOUR HEART (1 JOHN 1:8 – 2:2; 2:15-17)

THE PATTERN OF THIS WORLD WORKSHEET

Read I John I:8 – 2:2. We are all sinful, but what does God promise to do? What does Jesus do?

Read I John 2:15-17. What are we not to do? What are the sort of things that verse 16 defines as worldly?

Where do these things come from?

What two reasons does John give for not loving the world?

Apply:

What sort of things are we tempted to love that are worldly?

Are these things permanent or temporary? Why do we crave them?

Which way is your heart pointing? (see Mark 10:17-31)

GOD AND YOUR MIND (ROMANS 11:32–12:2)

THE PATTERN OF THIS WORLD WORKSHEET

Read Romans 11:32 – 12:2.
Why does Paul begin 12:1 with 'therefore'?

What are we to do in response to God's love and salvation?

Why do you think that Paul talks about our minds being transformed? What might he mean?

Why are our minds so important that Paul calls for transforming them as the first part of becoming a 'living sacrifice'?

Apply:

Who is in control of your mind? How will you know if you are still controlling your mind?

What sort of things do we allow into our minds? How can we filter these things practically?

Consider the following quotation, attributed to Ralph Waldo Emerson:

> Sow a thought and you reap an action;
> sow an act and you reap a habit;
> sow a habit and you reap a character;
> sow a character and you reap a destiny.

How does it describe the descent from mere thoughts to addictive behaviour?

What addictions might we need to be careful of, regarding the media that surrounds us the whole time?

GOD AND YOUR EYES (LUKE 11:29-36)

THE PATTERN OF THIS WORLD WORKSHEET

Read Luke 11:29-32.

To whom is Jesus likening himself? What was the original response from the Ninevites in particular?

Read 11:33-36.

Jesus describes his teaching as a lamp. What should happen to a lamp and why? How should we treat Jesus' teaching?

What might Jesus mean when he says that the eye is the lamp of the body, in the context of talking about how we treat his teaching?

Apply:

How might knowing our Bibles really well help us when we face the temptation of looking at the wrong sorts of material?

What practical ways can you think of to help each other live a Christian life in a society so full of visual images, many of which are unhelpful?

The internet. Never before have people had such a powerful visual tool at their disposal. What are the particular dangers for Christians in all this visual content?

GOD AND YOUR WORDS (COLOSSIANS 4:2-6, EPHESIANS 4:25-29; 5:4)

THE PATTERN OF THIS WORLD WORKSHEET

Read Colossians 4:2-6.

For what is Paul asking prayer? What sort of proclamation is Paul emphasising?

How should we present ourselves to others? What does this mean in practice?

Read Ephesians 4:25-29; 5:4.

Make two lists of the sort of talk Paul is condemning and what he is encouraging. Discuss which things on the list are difficult to stop or start and which are easy.

Apply:

Are there any conversations that you should not take part in? Are you ready for the consequences of being different in the way you speak?

What behaviour do you need to change regarding your online or text conversations? What practical ways can you think of together that will help them to be full of grace and seasoned with salt?

GOD AND YOUR HANDS (PROVERBS 6:6-11)

THE PATTERN OF THIS WORLD WORKSHEET

Read Proverbs 6:6-11.

What is it about the ant that lazy people need to consider? (v.6-8)

What temptation is faced by the sluggard? (v.9-10)

What are the consequences of behaving like a sluggard? (v.11)

How might we fall into the traps and end up doing what we shouldn't?

Apply:

Read Proverbs 12:11. How might 'chasing fantasies' be a trap we might fall into on the internet?

Work, Rest and Play in the Bible

Read Genesis 2:15. What is Adam to do in the Garden of Eden? Is this a surprise?

Read Exodus 20:8-10. Why do you think that the people needed reminding about God's rest after creation?

Apply:

Read Colossians 3:22-24. What are 'slaves' (workers) told to do and why?

Read 1 Thessalonians 4:11-12. What other reasons do we have for working hard?

How might you need to change the way you think about work? What challenge do you face regarding the way you spend time on the internet?

GOD AND YOUR LIFE (EPHESIANS 5:1-16)

THE PATTERN OF THIS WORLD WORKSHEET

Read Ephesians 5:1-2.

As Christians, what is our new status with God?

Read Ephesians 5:3-16.

What were we once and what are we now? (v.8)

What are the attributes of light and darkness? (v.9-14)

Light	Darkness

How does Paul contrast our lives now with what they once were? (v.15-16)

Apply:

Think about some of the attributes of 'light'. What might these mean for us and our lives?

Read Ephesians 5:3-7.

What are the implications for us as we try to put the above things into action? What do you think 'not even a hint' means?

What changes might you need to make to your lifestyle to ensure that every compartment belongs to God and that you obey him, even when there is no one else around?